Understanding the Dynamics of Dog Interaction

Nikki Ivey

DEDICATION

This book is dedicated to all those dog lovers who have chosen to educate themselves on developing dogs to their full potential. May the information in this book give you the skills you need to be successful in your job.

CONTENTS

Chapter 1
The Importance of Understanding Dog Interaction

Whether you work with dogs professionally, foster dogs regularly or have your own pack at home, this book with give you the knowledge to develop your dog's potential to be the dog he was born to be.

The goal of this book is to teach you how to help your dog interact appropriately with other dogs. Whether greeting or disagreeing, you will learn what behaviors are appropriate and acceptable for your dog to exhibit, and how to handle behaviors that are not appropriate.

Dogs must interact with one another in order to learn the proper dog communication skills to help them avoid conflict. When humans misunderstand dog interaction, it can be detrimental to the success and development of a dog. Often, we humans interrupt interaction prematurely or too often, not allowing dogs to develop important communication skills. Our own fears can lead to frustrated dogs, and can promote behavioral issues such as a lack of self-control, dog aggression, fear or anxiety.

As an owner and leader, you have the ability to help dogs improve the way they interact with one another, therefore improving their communication skills.

Interaction promotes good behavior throughout the dog's life, not just during playtime with a buddy. Through interaction dogs improve upon their communication skills, their ability to adjust play, enhance their self-control and build confidence. All of this helps them to be a better dog.

Dogs begin interacting with one another the moment they are born. From birth to two week of age, most interaction is with the mother through feeding and cleaning. As their auditory, olfactory and visual senses develop, puppies begin interacting more with their littermates. They begin barking, walking and wagging, and begin teaching one another how to be dogs. During interaction, the puppies learn about play, bite inhibition and hierarchy, and will improve their physical coordination. By seven weeks of age, puppies have full use of their senses, and will begin to play rougher with littermates. This is why a patient adult dog plays such an integral role in a puppy's life at this time.

At 8 weeks of age, puppies go through a fear period. It is crucial puppies experience positive interaction with other dogs during this time. This allows they puppy to develop communication skills that are essential for appropriate interactions with other dogs.

Dogs should have the opportunity to play with many different types of dogs, each varying in personality, age and size. This will help the dog to learn the difference between appropriate and inappropriate play and communication signals.

"A well-developed dog is one who has been socialized positively with dogs, humans and other species of animals." -Nikki Ivey

Chapter 2
Dog Communication: Foundation of Interaction

In order to understand how dogs interact, you must first understand how and why they communicate. Dog language is the utilization of specific body postures, noises and actions that help a dog communicate effectively with other dogs and people. A dog's sole purpose for using dog language is to avoid conflict. Dogs perceive conflict differently than humans. Dogs may perceive conflict or stress when another dog or human plays too rough, when a human, animal or object approaches too quickly, or when a human is loud or overly confrontational. Conflict can also be caused by elements in the environment such as thunder, fireworks, cameras or cars. Avoiding conflict does not always mean a dog is trying to thwart a fight; it means he is trying to pacify himself and/or whatever makes him uncomfortable. Dogs need to learn how to appropriately communicate with other dogs and, conversely, humans need to know how to read this language.

Conflict can arise during any type of interaction. A dog's use of appropriate language skills can help keep interaction with others conflict-free. As the dog's leader, it is your responsibility to understand communication signals in order to keep interaction appropriate and respectful. Knowing communication signals will allow you to evaluate dogs and communicate clearly with them.

Calming Signals

There are **three levels of calming signals dogs use in order to communicate**. These levels range from passive (Level 1) to aggressive (Level 3). Dog language can be difficult to detect and decipher until you are introduced to it.

Dogs offer a *behavior* when they want something, like a treat, a toy or play. They offer a *signal* when they want to solicit a calming effect.

<u>Level 1 – Passive Signals</u>

Level 1 is the most innate level of signals used, but *only if* the dog has had a chance to practice dog language. Many dogs lack proficient communication skills because they do not get adequate interaction with other dogs. Although born with the ability to communicate, dogs must practice these skills on a regular basis. If not, they lack the confidence to control a situation that may escalate into conflict. Dogs with insufficient language skills usually skip Level 1 signals.

Head Turn:

This is the most commonly used signal. A dog will slowly turn his head from side to side, avoiding eye contact. He may do this for many seconds before attempting another signal in order to give the conflict a chance to appropriately diminish. You probably see this signal often when trying to photograph a dog because many dogs see cameras as a conflict. You can use this signal to calm a dog that is nervous, shy or overly excited.

Body Turn:

A dog will turn his entire body from a frontal position and show you his side or he may turn all the way around and show you his rear. This is another great signal that you can use to help calm down a dog. This is the most effective technique when dealing with a jumping dog.

Eye Aversion:

This is when a dog will avert his eyes away from you without necessarily turning his head or body. You will often see dogs do this when you have a dog's face in your hands, and he cannot turn his head.

Sit:

Dogs will sit when dealing with a new dog, an overly excited dog or a human who is being too forceful. Many times a sit will become a default behavior when a dog does not know what else to do to appease a situation. To understand if the action is a signal or a behavior, look at the rest of the body. If it is used as a signal, the dog will use it with another signal like turning the head or averting the eyes. If it is a behavior, the dog will sit and look towards the other dog or human. This is a great signal to use when dealing with nervous or shy dogs. Instead of sitting, I recommend squatting so it is easier to move away or closer to the dog depending on the response he is giving you. When you squat, you will always use another signal like head turning, body turning or averting the eyes.

Down:

This signal is not as common as the previous. Little dogs are more likely to use the down as a signal or behavior than a larger dog. Dogs with a high level of confidence will also be more likely to use this signal. Like a sit, you will see other behaviors combined with it. Always look at the rest of the body and in what context the down is being used.

Bow:

This can be used as a signal or as a behavior. When used as a signal, a dog will go into the bow position where his front legs are stretched out in front and his bottom is up in the air. However, unlike a play bow where a dog will jump from side-to-side quickly as a play invitation, a dog will remain stationary when using a bow as a calming signal. When it is a signal, you will often times see it mixed with another signal like averting eyes or turning the head. Dogs that have very good dog skills will sometimes use a bow as a signal and behavior at the same time. He may want another dog to play, but if the other dog is anxious, the bowing dog may offer a calming signal to relieve the tension of the encounter. You can use this as a signal yourself, but you may feel silly doing it. I recommend using the more natural signals like head and body turns, eye aversion and sitting/squatting.

Quick Licks:

This signal is difficult to see until you are used to spotting it. A quick lick is when the tongue comes out of the mouth and in a very quick motion licks the nose and then quickly moves back in. A dog that uses this will do it several times in a row to try and get his point across. Quick licks will also be combined with other signals.

Raised Paw:

This signal is not used as often as the others. When a dog is using this as a signal, he will slightly raise the paw and use another signal with it. Keep in mind you must read the entire body in order to identify this as a calming signal. If the dog is a pointer, for instance, a raised paw may mean the dog is simply pointing something.

Doing Something Else (Ignoring):

A dog will do this when he wants to extinguish a behavior. He may sniff the ground, urinate and/or completely ignore what it is he wants to extinguish. Many people see this as a dog being stubborn but in most cases, the dog is trying to calm a situation. For example, your dog, Jake, is playing in the yard and you call him to you. He does not listen to you the first three times. Why? He may not know the command. Or, if he does, you could be using a harsh tone that he views as a conflict. If the latter is correct, Jake will ignore you and wait for you to calm down.

Yawning:

Dogs yawn for two reasons. He may yawn because he is tired or as a signal to calm a situation or himself. Look at what context the yawn is being used to help you decide if it is a signal or a behavior. On occasion, a dog will use this with other signals.

Curving:

When meeting a new dog or sometimes, a new person, a dog will curve towards the object to show calmness and friendliness. This is where dogs will greet one another by smelling their rear ends or genitalia. This seems rude to us, but in reality, meeting face-to-face is inappropriate and confrontational in a dog's world. Many dogs, especially puppies, are not good at this signal due to a lack of experience and maturity. Poor greeting signals will often start a scuffle. Use this method when meeting a new dog. Walking up to the dog from the side, and curving to greet him. Do not approach a strange dog from the front. And I suggest that you never bend over a dog that you are unfamiliar with its personality.

Splitting Up:

If you have ever had a dog sit or stand between you and another person, (i.e. while cuddling on the couch with your significant other), you have probably seen this signal. Many people think this is a cute gesture of jealousy, however the dog actually sees this as a conflict and is trying to *literally* split you apart. During play, dogs will do this when they sense other dogs' rough play will cause a fight. Confident, experienced dogs will walk between two dogs, and will stay with the offending dog until it redirects, much like an umpire during a sporting match. This signal takes a lot of practice as most dogs lack the consistency, confidence and follow-through to do it properly. The more a dog has a chance to interact with other dogs, the better he will become.

Level 2 - Less Passive Signals

Level 2 signals are less passive and very easily recognized. Many humans become uncomfortable when they see Level 2 signals, often labeling a dog as vicious. Dogs will use Level 2 signals if they do not have confidence, time to use Level 1 signals, or to articulate to the other dog that his patience is growing thin.

Growling:

A dog will give a low growl to let another dog or person know he is uncomfortable. This means that the dog is *trying* to control a potentially conflicting situation. When growling is used as a signal it is mixed with other signals such as a head turn. If growling is a behavior, other signals are not used, and the dog's posture will be stiff and he will stare at the person or dog ahead of him. If you have a patient dog with good dog language, he will often try Level 1 signals first. If using Level 1 signals is not effective, he will be forced to escalate to Level 2. For example, if a family pet is constantly harassed by a child at home, (say the child is crawling all over him, chasing him down, getting in his face, etc.), and the dog's Level 1 signals are being ignored, the dog will be forced to escalate to Level 2. When the dog growls at the child, the family scolds the dog instead of educating the child, or they improperly assume the dog is vicious, and re-home the dog or worse. This scenario is one that occurs all too often. It is important to know whether the dog had previously displayed Level 1 signals prior to the growl, and before jumping to Level 2.

Snarling:

A snarl occurs when a dog pulls his lips up and shows his teeth. This signal is often used with a low growl and always with a Level 1 signal such as a quick lick, head turn or eye aversion. Many fearful dogs with no confidence will resort to this behavior immediately when faced with an uncomfortable situation. Dogs with confidence will use a snarl if they do not have time to use a Level 1 signal, (i.e. when another dog is suddenly in his face). Like the growl, if it is not mixed with other signals, it is being given as a behavior with the possibility of turning into aggression.

Level 3 – Aggressive Signals

Level 3 is considered the Aggressive Level. When a dog uses Level 3 signals, it does not mean he is vicious or is an aggressive dog, it just means that the signals are much more noticeable to the untrained eye. Dogs use this Level when Levels 1 and 2 did not work or he does not have the patience or skills to do Levels 1 and 2 first. Level 3 signals are very obvious and often make people nervous. Because of their lack of understanding, they will often punish or correct a dog for offering Level 3 signals. This will normally make the dog resort to level 3 faster than usual, because of the association of correction or punishment when another dog gets too close. Level 3 signals can also be behaviors from a dog that is being a bully so you must read the dog's entire body to understand.

Muzzle Grab:

A muzzle grab occurs when a dog attempts to place his mouth over another dog's muzzle. This may be a sign of dominance because it places another dog into a submissive position. Humans sometimes use a version of this by purchasing head halters that go over the muzzle of their dog. This is placed into the aggressive level, because there is physical contact between the dogs. Though the dog giving signals does not intend to cause harm, the dog receiving the muzzle grab will oftentimes get a cut on the bridge of the muzzle because the skin is thin in this area. This behavior is acceptable when the previous two levels have not worked. Most young puppies experience this at least once in their life. If you observe a dog is not respecting Level 1 and 2 signals, you should correct the disrespectful dog—not the dog giving the signals.

Snapping:

When giving this signal a dog will snap towards whatever needs calming, and then back away quickly. This occurs when humans who do not understand that the dog has been displaying Level 1 and 2 signals and continue to place the dog in an uncomfortable and stressful environment. When the conflict is not resolved, then the dog will escalate to snapping. A dog at this level is usually snapping out of fear, or lacks the confidence and maturity to disengage emotionally from what is causing the fear. Essentially, all he wants is to avoid conflict and to make something go away. The dog that uses snapping as a behavior, will often not back down after snapping. This is the difference between a dog using proper dog language or getting caught up in his fear turning dangerously aggressive. This is also the number one signal that is used when a dog has no confidence or does not understand the first two levels.

Biting:

Often times biting is a dog's last resort when other signals have not worked. Like a dog that uses a snap, dogs with low confidence or language skills often bite instead of offering Level 1 or 2 signals. If a dog is using this as a signal, the dog will often bite and then back off. I define a bite as a snap with contact. A signal bite is different than a warning bite. A dog that is using the bite as a warning behavior will hold and shake its victim and not back down. A hold and shake will cause more damage than a signal bite and release.

When observing any Level 3 signals, you must not jump to conclusions. Level 3 signals do not necessarily mean that the dog is vicious and cannot be rehabilitated. You must evaluate the dog carefully to adequately evaluate why the dog used this level of signals or behavior. Is he offering Level 1 and 2 first or is he going immediately to Level 3? The more you observe, the more competent you will be at evaluating the dog.

Various Signals

Dogs give other dogs and humans various signals that help them communicate. These signals are not necessarily calming signals, and are typically easy to recognize.

Tail Wag:

This is the most misunderstood signal. A tail wag does not always mean "happy dog". A tail wag means a dog is aroused in one form or another. When evaluating what a particular tail wag means look at the entire body for confirmation. Also, take a dog's breed into consideration. Many dogs do not have tails, and others normally have a stiff or curled tail.

If a dog's tail is **slow and relaxed**, the dog is comfortable in the current situation. I also refer to this as the "flag" wag, because it often looks like a flag blowing in the wind.

A **high, stiff and slow wag** means the dog is being challenging or taking a defensive posture. If it is not moving, the dog could be trying to calm another dog. I refer to this wag as a "stick in low wind."

A **high, stiff and fast wag** means a dog is highly aroused. Arousal can come from a variety of sources. This is also known as the "stick in a hurricane" wag.

A fast to moderate and relaxed wags means a dog is happy and comfortable. Often times the wag will make a circle, which is why I refer to this as a "circle wag."

If a dog has a **low/no wag,** the dog is uncomfortable from fear or nervousness. A low/no wag can also come from pain. Sometimes the tail will be tucked between the legs.

Raised Hackles:

At some point you will see the fur on the back or neck of a dog stand up. This is a natural response to arousal. Arousal can be from excitement, being unsure, low confidence, and/or aggression. A dog that has his hackles raised is not necessarily getting ready to attack. You must always read the entire body of a dog to really understand what he is trying to communicate. Again, you must be aware of the breed. Breeds such as Rhodesian ridgebacks have raised fur all the time.

Shake Off:

Shake offs are used as a "release" which can denote the beginning of play or the end of a sequence of events, (i.e. after a long introduction, a dog shakes off to show he is ready for play).

Barking:

Dog use barking as a vocal way to communicate. Keep in mind a mastiff and a Chihuahua will have different low-pitched barks:

A **high-pitched bark** indicates excitement, heavy arousal, fearfulness or nervousness.

A **low-pitched bark** is used for warning or frustration.

Distance Increasing Signals

These signals are used to increase the distance between a dog and a conflict. When a dog is uncomfortable with something (i.e. another dog that is too close), he will use these signals as a way to express his desire to be away from the conflict.

Whining, Yelping and Crying:

These will often come from insecure puppies or dogs that are unable to use calming signals properly. Crying and whining is a vocal way of demonstrating frustration and not used for distance increasing. Yelping can be associated with pain, (think about the last time you accidentally stepped on your dog's tail).

Humans Can Speak Dog

Humans are capable of communicating with dogs by using these same signals. Whether you have a dog that is afraid, nervous or outgoing, you can calm him by using these same signals. Practice using these signals with your own dog until they become second nature to you. Start by seeing how well your dog responds to them. How well they respond will tell you how well they know dog language, as well as help you improve your own skills. **Use only Level 1 signals** with dogs and be sure to be confident and consistent!

A **head turn** is easy to use with a jumping or nervous dog. Be sure to completely ignore the dog (no touching or talking) while using this signal.

A **body turn** is a great way to deal with a jumping dog. When the dog sits for 3-5 seconds, verbally acknowledge the dog for being good. If the dog jumps again, turn your body and ignore him. If the dog is causing you pain from jumping, ignore the dog and walk to another room.

Use a **sit or squat** with a nervous or fearful dog (if they are not oversized.) Always keep your body turned to the side.

In order for **yawning** to work, you must be consistent. Mix this with another signal such as a head turn. You can use this signal to your advantage when dealing with a nervous or shy dog. For instance, if a dog is afraid of thunderstorms, make sure the dog is near you. Simply ignore the dog (do not coddle), and yawn from time to time. You may see the dog begin to yawn back. He is trying to calm himself.

Again**, curving** should always be used when meeting a new dog. Approach the dog from the side, and curve to greet. Do not approach a dog head on.

Split-ups should not be overused. It is essential that you are confident and consistent when walking in between two dogs. Follow-though is crucial in order for this signal to work. For example, if your dog is barking at a door, confidently position yourself between the dog and the door. Move your body toward the dog until it redirects. Do not talk or touch the dog. If the dog gets around you and returns to the door, do not panic. Simply start over. To associate a command with this technique, use the phrase "that's enough" before performing the slit up. This technique can be used to interrupt a variety of inappropriate behaviors.

Chapter 3
Understanding Dog Interaction

Again, dogs must interact in order to learn and practice proper dog communication skills to help them avoid conflict. Misunderstanding dog interaction can be detrimental to the success of a dog's development. By not understanding appropriate behavior, many owners interrupt dogs too often. This can lead to frustrated dogs, and can also promote behavior issues such as a lack of self-control, dog aggression, fear or anxiety.

Types of Interaction

There are three different types of interactions that occur between dogs: Greetings, play and altercations.

1. Greetings

There are two steps to the greeting process. The first is the approach. During the initial approach dogs should begin communicating by curving, and turning their heads and bodies. They should approach slowly, allowing the other dog to receive, respect and respond to the signals given. By approaching appropriately the dogs have a higher chance of getting along. If a dog approaches incorrectly, (by running straight up to another dog), a negative first impression could be made, and an altercation could occur. Many dogs have a difficult time with this process due to a lack of communication skills and self-control.

The second step in the greeting process is the introduction. The introduction begins when the dogs get within touching distance of one another. Their bodies should remain in a curved fashion. They will then approach each other on the backside for a sniff. This is how they get to know each other. This process should occur with the initial greeting only and does not have to be repeated if the dogs know each other. Once this step is completed, the greeting is over and the next step in interaction can begin. As a supervisor, you should praise appropriate skills during the both steps of the greeting process.

2. Play

Dogs initiate play in seven different ways. Some of these may be combined to increase the chances that he will get a positive response.

1. **Lying on Back:** Dogs will often times roll over to expose their bellies when initiating play. The purpose is not to bow down to the other dog but to show a submissive attitude. By doing this, the dog initiating is hoping to relax the receiving dog enough to get play started.

2. **Offering A Toy:** Dogs use toys on a regular basis to offer play-both with humans and dogs. They may put the toy in

the face of another dog to tempt him to play tug. They will also play keep-a-way to in order to initiate a game of chase.

3. **Nudging:** This is where a dog will take his nose and poke the other dog. They will typically poke along the neck and shoulder area. This nudging action is considered rude if the other dog is ignoring or offering other calming signals, and the dog initiating play ignores these signals or nudges harder. In these instances, you will interrupt the dog who is being rude.

4. **Paw Tap:** A paw tap is used similar to nudging except the dog will use his paw. Your own dog may do this to you at home while you are sitting on the couch, and he hopes to gain your attention. Just as with nudging, if the dog offering this behavior does not respect the signals of a dog who does not want to play, you must interrupt.

5. **Play Bow:** This is the most common and recognizable initiation of play. This occurs when a dog stretches his front feet out and has his rear in the air. This differs from a calming bow or just a stretch in that he will also be bouncing from side to side in front of the dog with whom he wants to play.

6. **Barking:** This initiation will often be mixed with the other offers of play, such as the play bow. This behavior can become excessive and disrespectful if the other dog is trying to ignore or walk away from him.

7. **Whining:** Similar to barking, this behavior will be mixed with other offers to play.

Play Styles:

Once play has been initiated, dogs will play in one of four play <u>styles:</u>

1. **Wrestling:** Two or three dogs will be often times stationary with one on the bottom and the other two bouncing around and playing on top. This can be mixed with the chase game as well. Wrestling is the type of play that is often misunderstood by humans. They often see this as aggressive play that needs to be interrupted. You must always look at the dogs that are involved and what the rest of their body is telling you. The dog that is on the bottom is often times the one that is in charge of the game and controls when the game begins and when it ends. Periodically, you will see wrestling occur while both dogs are standing.

2. **Chasing:** Multiple dogs will often be involved in this game. This is a great game, but must be supervised well. Small dogs may get injured by big dogs who are not watching where they are going. Occasionally, you will also notice one or more dogs trying to calm the game by using the split-up technique. The dog being chased is the dog in charge and in control.

3. **Tug:** This is a great game between two dogs who are not competing for a position in the pack. If it is a game for fun, you will see relaxed bodies from both dogs and when one lets go, the other will tease the dog with the toy to initiate play again. A third dog that is trying to split up the behavior to avoid potential conflict will sometimes interrupt this game. When a third dog attempts to play tug with the two, conflict may arise. Tug is something that should never be done between a human and a dog when there are multiple dogs around.

4. **Boxing:** This game is normally played by two dogs that stand on their back legs and "box" with each other. This game may also be interrupted by a third dog attempting to split up the behavior.

Mounting

Though this behavior seems inappropriate and embarrassing to humans, it is very normal and natural for dogs. Interruption is on a per-case basis.

All dogs, regardless of sex or alteration may mount. There are **three different types of mounting**.

1. **Arousal:** This occurs when a dog becomes too excited. Mounting is very brief and has little meaning. Mounting will usually occur on the backside or flank area. There is no need to interrupt this behavior, as it will dissipate quickly. The dog mounting is never "pushy" towards the other dog. However, this mounting behavior can turn into sexual mounting.

2. **Sexual:** This is a natural behavior that dogs do regardless of sex or alteration. A dog can be "pushy" when doing this and will sometimes disregard any signals coming from the dog he is mounting. This is when the dog has become "fixated" and must be interrupted. Sexual mounting will be more precise on the backside or on the flank by young puppies. You will see a penis extension and possibly swelling. Humping can continue after dog has dismounted. This behavior

can also turn into dominant mounting.

3. **Dominant:** This mounting can occur at any time. It can be very "pushy" and can become aggressive if the mounted dog does not submit. However, I do not interrupt this play unless you see the dominant dog taking advantage of the submissive dog or if the mounted dog becomes aggressive. This can turn into sexual once dominance has been established.

Inappropriate Behavior

There are many inappropriate behaviors that should not be allowed during dog interaction. By being conscientious of these behaviors, you can interrupt them before they cause altercations.

A dog **disrespecting other dogs' signals** is the most common inappropriate behavior you will run into. This may be a dog that wants to play and is not backing off a dog that does not want to play. I always allow a couple of minutes before interrupting to give the dogs a chance to work it out themselves. You can interrupt this behavior with a verbal ("that's enough") and/or by using the split-up technique. If a dog becomes a bully, or is fixated on a particular dog, you may have to implement a time-out.

Resource guarding can be a problem that needs to be interrupted immediately. Dogs need to understand that all things belong to you, and their role is not to guard that resource. Dog may resource guard the pool, toys, space, gate, other dogs or the water bowl.

Excessively rough play can initiate altercations. If both dogs are being equal participants, do not interrupt, however, if one dog is being too rough and lacks self-control, you may have to interrupt. There is a good chance that the dog will not slow down long enough to read any signals that may be given to him by his playmate.

Uninvited play occurs when a dog approaches two or more dogs who are playing. He will attempt to become part of the play. If the group of dogs playing allows him to join, there is nothing for you to do. However, if they spend time ignoring him or pause play due to his presence, you will need to interrupt. Allow the dog to read and respond the group's signals before interrupting.

Excessive mounting is an inappropriate behavior if the dog becomes fixated or becomes pushy or aggressive.

Tagging is a behavior that can be mixed with rough or uninvited play. Tagging occurs when a dog uses his mouth to "tag" a dog on the back of the neck. Sometimes tagging can occur on other parts of the body. This behavior should be interrupted immediately.

Fixation can occur with play or mounting. This behavior exists when a dog is disrespecting signals of another dog, and will not leave the dog alone. This behavior will need to be interrupted immediately. Typically this behavior must be interrupted with a time-out.

Indirect Aggression is the most serious inappropriate behavior as it can cause harm to you or other dogs. Indirect aggression occurs when a dog gets excited about something but is unable to obtain it. In order to release his frustration over not getting the item he wants, he may release this energy on a nearby human or dog by attacking it. For example, a dog that is not allowed to have a tennis ball may get frustrated and attack something else like you or another dog. A dog may also get too excited when other dogs are jumping on a human or barking at another dog through a fence and it results in indirect aggression. Be very aware of the dogs that you have in the group and which ones may reach that excited state too quickly, get frustrated and lash out. Indirect aggression is a real problem that can occur so quickly that it usually ends up in a fight.

Interrupting Inappropriate Behavior

When supervising dog interaction you want to do the least amount of work as possible, as you want dogs to work conflict out themselves. In the beginning, you may have to be more involved, but once you have helped your dog learn appropriate interaction skills you will find that there will be less work for you.

When interrupting inappropriate behavior, you will first give a verbal. This verbal will be the name of the dog followed by "that's enough." Stay calm and matter-of-fact when giving this command. If your dog does not understand what this command means, you will give the command while using the split-up technique. Be sure to stay consistent until the dog redirects himself from the dog or object. For example, if a dog is mounting another dog inappropriately and is disrespecting another dog's signals, start by giving a verbal "that's enough." If the dog does not know what this means, or is fixated on the other dog, you will physically position yourself between the two dogs. Face the dog who is being disrespectful, and begin to walk towards him. Do this without touching the dog. Continue to do this until he redirects himself by walking away. If you have to do three split-ups in a row, go to the next level, which is time-out on leash. Put the dog on leash and make him stand beside me for at least one minute before being allowed free again. If you have to do the on-leash time-out three times, he needs to be removed from the play area for a time-out. This time-out is also about one minute. If you have to do this time-out three times, playtime should end for the time being.

The purpose of the interruption is to communicate to the dog that inappropriate behavior means attention and playtime will end. Having good timing when giving verbal warnings or time-outs is crucial so you can communicate to the dog exactly which action they did that is not acceptable. Be patient and be consistent as it may take multiple tries to communicate which behaviors are inappropriate.

3. Altercations

Altercations and disagreements occur during interaction and cannot be completely avoided. Understand that this is a risk that all owners must take into consideration, but that most altercations can be avoided. Dogs have altercations for various reasons. It can be that a dog is tired or grumpy, is being disrespectful of another dog's signals, or it could be that two dogs just do not get along.

Not every altercation is going to cause harm nor is it going to need to be interrupted. Each altercation will be different based on the dogs involved and what precipitated prior to the altercation.

There are four different types of altercations:

1. **Accidental:** A dog may get too rough or excited during play causing another dog to yelp, whine or cry. This is typically over very quickly. Think about the last time you played Twister or any similar, physical game. If someone accidentally steps on your foot, you may wince or yell out, but you are likely to forgive quickly and resume play.

Dogs react in this same way, and will resume play after a shake off.

2. **Warning:** This occurs when a dog is being too rough during play because of a lack of control. This may cause the irritated dog to bark, growl or snap. This will sound like a fight but is usually very quick lived and dissipates quickly. Dogs may separate themselves and find other playmates for a period. You will only need to interrupt if the dog lacking self-control continues to play too rough, and does not respect the dog who has used Level 2 signals.

3. **Argument:** This altercation is much louder than the warning. This will often have body contact, growling, snarling and snapping. Arguments do not have mouth to body contact and real harm is not intended. When over each dog will typically separate for a long period. Interruption is on a per case basis. If an interruption is needed then a verbal should be enough.

4. **Fight:** There are various reasons why fights occur. Usually a fight will sound worse than it really is. Dogs will usually fight in a boxing or wrestling fashion. Sometimes they will end without your interruption. There are three levels of fight:

1. This fight will typically have mouth to skin contact. However, there are no injuries, only slobber.
2. This fight will have mouth to skin contact with scrapes or cuts but no real wounds.
3. This fight will have mouth to skin contact and will result in puncture wounds. These injuries may require veterinary care.

Within any of these fights you will typically have injuries around the neck and head area.

There are fights that do not fit in any of these levels. If a dog injures another dog with multiple injuries, veterinary care and the injuries were not isolated to the head and neck area then we must look at the dog as truly being aggressive and attempting to do serious harm. A dog that has been involved in this type of fight should not be allowed around other dogs until professional help has been called in.

Interrupting a Fight

There may be times to when it is impossible to prevent a fight from occurring. Knowing how to calmly and confidently break up a fight will increase the chances of everyone remaining safe and injury free.

As a leader, you must remain calm, confident and matter-of-fact. You should never let your emotions show, even if you are nervous.

The first step will be a verbal ("that's enough"). Use the same tone you would use when interrupting inappropriate behavior. You may have to raise your volume but only if the dogs are being loud themselves. If the verbal does not work you will need to separate the dogs. This must be done carefully so you do not become injured as the result of indirect aggression from either dog.

If you have one initiator and one receiver then you should be able to grab the back legs or under the haunches of the initiator. Gently pull him backwards and move him sideways so he loses balance and becomes distracted. Do this slowly and gently so the dog cannot rip the skin of the other dog. If both dogs are initiating the fight, then two people should be available to separate the dogs. Physically separating the dogs should be done after the verbal. Never attempt to pull dogs apart while mouths are attached to skin as this can cause more damage. If you are physically unable to separate you may use an object to place between the two dogs such as a chair. You may also use one quick blast from an air horn. Do not use any adversive techniques such as a water hose or objects that could cause physical harm to the dogs such as hitting or whipping. After the dogs are separated, put them in a time-out in order to allow them to calm down.

Chapter 4
Understanding Dog Personality

There are many attributes of a dog's life that can and will affect the way a dog interacts. Genes, upbringing, personality and breed can all have an effect on how well your dog interacts with other dogs.

A dog has two sets of genes, one from each parent. Those genes effect, not only physical attributes, but physiological attributes such as a dogs susceptibility of getting ill. A dog that suffers from chronic illnesses will be affected in how well he interacts with others. A dog can also be passed an "aggressive" trait that will cause the dog many issues. Fortunately, there are more important attributes, ones that you can control and modify that will play a more important role in your dog's interactive future.

Personality

It is important that you understand what makes up a dog's personality so you can assist in his full development. A dog's personality is made up of six different attributes. You can attempt to modify a dog's personality by improving on each individual attribute, though there are some dogs who cannot be modified due to hereditary issues.

1. Temperament: This is the "attitude" the dog is born with. Most temperaments can be modified through proper training. Knowing a dog's temperament will also give you a good idea as to what type of player he may be.

1. **Dominant-** A dog with a dominant temperament is a natural leader. This dog will control a situation if allowed to do so. If this dog is challenged for the leadership role by a weaker, non-consistent pack member, he may become difficult to deal with. It is important that this dog has a consistent leader (you). Dominant dogs are not always aggressive, just more forceful. These dogs are similar to natural born leaders within the human race.

2. **Submissive-**A submissive dog submits to a leader with little argument. He is comfortable in the role he has been placed in within the pack, and does not mind being a follower. If the pack leader is inconsistent, he may attempt to take over, however, this often stresses the dog out until leadership from a human has been established. Dogs in this case can become nervous and lose confidence if no leader is present in the home.

3. **Fearful-** A fearful dog consistently has phobias such as being afraid of strangers, thunderstorms, new places, going

for a ride, being left alone, meeting new dogs, etc. He has a hard time adjusting to new, different and stressful situations. This dog will often flee from scary situations. If he is unable to flee, he may resort to Level II signals quickly, and may be deemed a "fear biter." This issue can be more problematic than dealing with a truly vicious dog in that this dog is often unpredictable. Confidence building exercises will help this dog learn to deal with fearful situations without resorting to fleeing or biting.

4. **Nervous**- A nervous dog has a hard time adjusting to new, different and stressful situations. He will often look to his owner for reassurance. He will more than likely not flee or snap but instead tries to hide behind objects or owner.

5. **Aggressive**- In this context, "aggressive" does not mean "forceful," it means "vicious." This dog is quick to snap or bite without warning, and will not back down. These dogs are difficult to work with and are often a danger to other dogs and people. Vicious dogs are usually born with this "seed." Occasionally this behavior can be modified when the dog is a puppy, but typically there is nothing that can be done to change this temperament. These dogs are often euthanized as they are a danger to society. Only a trained professional, knowledgeable in dog behavior, can appropriately deem a dog as aggressive or vicious. There

are often times underlying issues that explain the behavior of the dog. Fear aggression is often times misunderstood for aggression.

6. **Indifferent**: This is a dog who care nothing about what is going on around him. This is an unusual temperament for dogs because they are pack animals.

7. **Flexible**: This dog has an excellent temperament, as he is able to adjust quickly to new environments, people or dogs. He can be dominant or submissive depending on the situation, and does not mind being the leader or follower. He is aware of what is going on around him, and does well with controlling himself. Unfortunately, this is a rare temperament in dogs today, however, it is possible to assist dogs in becoming flexible through proper training and socialization.

General Recommendations: If dog is fearful or nervous, confidence building is the first step. Ensuring that he has an opportunity to interact with trustworthy dogs will also increase his ability to become a great communicator. Do not baby, coddle or reassure a fearful or nervous dog as this will reinforce the issue. This dog should not be isolated from other dogs but should be trained instead.

2. Play Type: A dog's playing ability or preference of play.

1. **Player A:** This dog loves to play with anything and anyone. He understands how to play with dogs. He knows when to be submissive and when to be dominant during play. This dog is a great candidate for regular interaction.

2. **Player B:** This dog prefers playing non-aggressively and only enjoys playing with dogs that are similar. This dog tends to shy away from rough play.

3. **Player C:** This dog is often described as a "bully." He plays well but tends to push his weight around. Often times if another dog challenges him, he will back down and show submissiveness. On occasion, a dog may continue to push his weight around possibly cause a problem. He is fine for interaction if he has a consistent and confident leader. His play can improve if trained properly.

4. **Player D:** This dog is very nervous and does not understand how to play with other dogs. These dogs often need training before interaction is attempted. When interaction begins it should be with a trustworthy dog, slowly increasing the number of dogs and personalities.

5. **Player E:** This dog is extremely fearful and often exhibits fear aggression. This dog must have training before attempting to interact with other dogs. This dog often exhibits leash reactivity when on walks.

6. **Player F:** This dog attacks other dogs for no reason and is not a good candidate for interaction until outside training has taken place. This dog may never be capable of interacting with others.

3. Dog Language Skill: This is the dog's ability to communicate effectively with other dogs and people. This will be linked directly with a dog's confidence level.

1. **Excellent-** This dog knows how to communicate effectively with other dogs. Does very well at calming situations down.

2. **Good-**This dog knows the basics of dog language. He does well with other dogs that know dog language but does not know how to communicate with dogs that are not good with dog language.

3. **Fair-** This dog knows a few dog language skills but does not know the appropriate time to use them. When dog uses a signal, he does not give the receiver enough time to

respond before moving to a higher, more aggressive level of communication.

4. **Poor:** This dog has no knowledge of dog language skills. This is unable to communicate effectively during stressful situations.

General Recommendations: Dogs that are not good with dog language need consistent practice with patient dogs who exhibit excellent communication skills.

4. Social skills: This shows how well socialized a dog is with people and other dogs. This is very important when considering how well a dog will interact with other dogs.

1. **Excellent:** This dog loves people and does not hesitate to have everyone pet him. He enjoys being around other dogs.

2. **Good:** This dog likes most people, but may be a little weary of people who are not dog lovers or who are noticeably afraid of dogs. He does well with dogs who are friendly but may not do well with dogs who are nervous or afraid.

3. **Fair:** This dog only likes people and dogs he is familiar with. He takes a while to warm up to new people and dogs.

4. **Poor:** This is not social with people or dogs except for his own pack.

General Recommendations: If you have a dog that is Fair or Poor, you need to be sure to use good dog language skills to help him feel as comfortable as he can. Do not force this dog to be petted and do not try to encourage the dog to approach strange people or dogs. Confidence building exercises will prepare the dog in becoming more social. This dog should not be isolated from other dogs but should be trained instead.

5. Confidence: Confidence affects most areas of a dog's life and personality. A dog with low confidence will have a nervous or fearful temperament and will most likely be a Player D or E. A dog with confidence issues will have trouble problem solving and will not have great dog language skills.

1. **High:** This dog is able to handle different and stressful situations without a problem. He is not afraid to try or learn new things.

2. **Moderate:** This dog is able to handle different and stressful situations with a minimal amount of nervousness or stress. Dog has to be coaxed into trying or learning something new when out of his comfort zone. You will not see any problems from him when he is in his comfort zone.

3. **Low**- This dog has a hard time dealing with new, different and stressful situations. Dog must be coaxed to try or learn something new and even then, may still shut down. He will show small amounts of stress or nervousness even when in his comfort zone.

4. **None**: This dog is completely unable to handle new, different or stressful situations. He is nervous and stressed even in his comfort zone or home. He is unable to be coaxed to try or learn something new until confidence begins to build.

General Recommendations: Do not baby or coddle a dog if he has confidence issues. Always stay positive and refrain from ever using any type of corrections. Dogs with low confidence can still interact successfully with others. If a dog has no confidence, he needs some professional training to help build his confidence before returning to regular interaction. This dog should not be isolated from other dogs but should be trained instead.

6. Problem Solving Skill: A dog must be able to problem-solve in order to deal with conflicting situations. This is the hardest attribute to see naturally without doing some training exercises. This is not an attribute that you have to know in order to accurately determine a dog's true personality.

1. **Excellent:** This dog can take any situation and have the final outcome rule in their favor.

2. **Good:** This dog is good at problem solving during familiar situations, but struggles during new situations.

3. **Poor:** This dog has no ability to problem-solve in any situation. Has never been taught to use his brain.

Chapter 5
Human's Role in Development of their Dog's Interaction Ability

Dogs are inherently pack animals who need to interact with one another. From birth, they should be allowed to interact with dogs of different breeds, genders and sizes. If your dog currently has difficulty getting along with others, it is possible they can learn to interact appropriately. While your dog may not be able to or want to play with all dogs, he can learn to be in their presence without fear or aggression.

Unfortunately, we humans sometimes make mistakes when teaching our dogs appropriate behavior that can inhibit their ability to interact with others, and that can reinforce fears and dog aggressiveness.

Isolation is one of the biggest mistakes a dog owner can make. This often occurs because a puppy has not been fully vaccinated or due to other health concerns. It also occurs when a home has multiple dogs, and the owner believes this provides adequate socialization. Whatever the reason, it is essential for dogs of all ages to interact with others, even if there are multiple dogs in the home. Play dates with friends, day cares and dog parks provide great opportunities for socialization. Keep in mind it is rare for a dog to be truly anti-social If a dog is, he most likely has a behavioral issue.

Even when a dog is socialized regularly, it is important to ensure your dog is interacting appropriately and you are not interrupting inappropriately. If your dog is being disrespectful to another dog, it is your responsibility to interrupt correctly, with as little interaction and emotion as possible. Screaming, yelling or grabbing your dog in an aggressive manner will either escalate inappropriate behavior or will cause fear. Instilling fear in your dog when other dogs are around can cause dog aggression.

If you have found that your dog has developed dog aggression or leash reactivity due to your change of behavior when other dogs are around then you are going to need to deal with those issues with a trainer or dog behavioral consultant who uses positive training techniques. Meeting fear or aggression with harsh techniques will further fuel behavioral issues.

Fear and aggression can also be caused by a human interrupting play too quickly. Most of the time, dogs can work conflict out on their own. It is better for them to learn from other dogs than it is for them to learn primarily from us. With practice, you will learn when you should step in and when you should let a situation play out on its own.

A common inappropriate interruption occurs when a dog (especially a small breed) is picked up during play or conflict. Removing a dog in this way communicates fear and uncertainly as the dog learns that anytime another dog is his vicinity, the owner becomes anxious and inconsistent. It also does not allow him to learn to calm and control conflicts. If you worry about a large dog causing injury, allow your dog to play with larger adult dogs who have good communication skills. Keep in mind that all dogs communicate the same, just as a 4'5" human adult communicates the same way a 6'2" human adult does. You should allow your dog, regardless of size, to learn how to use the skills he was born with.

Anytime your dog interacts with others he should have your full attention. It is easy to get distracted with conversations and technology in a dog park, but for your dog's safety, it is important you focus on your dog at all times. Distracted owners often lose sight of their dogs, and get upset when he is involved in an altercation that could have been avoided. While you cannot control others' dogs, you can control your own. He counts on you to keep him safe and to be consistent when doing so.

Chapter 6
Safety Precautions

I encourage you to continue helping your dog interact with other dogs and humans. It is crucial to his development and should be taken seriously. There are many ways to get your dog the outside socialization that he needs. Day cares, play dates and dog parks are great outlets for this. Keep in mind the information you have learned as well as the following safety precautions in order to assist yourself and your dog in feeling comfortable with interaction and play:

Play Collars

I do not recommend allowing dogs to play while wearing their own collars. The collars can get damaged or can cause harm during play through choking. I recommend using breakaway collars or harnesses (during play only) on your dog. If you have good verbal control over you dog allowing him to play collar-free is ideal.

Taking Dogs into Play Areas

It is important dogs work for the opportunity to go into the play area in order to teach them self-control and problem-solving skills. This also helps you establish yourself as the leader of the group. You control all rewards, and entering a play area can definitely be a reward for your dog.

When you approach a play area with your dog ensure he is

exhibiting appropriate behavior by not jumping, barking or whining. If he is exhibiting any of these do not proceed to the next step. If you are in the car after pulling up to the dog park, sit quietly, ignoring him. Once he is exhibiting appropriate behavior for at least three seconds, you may begin the process.

Once you are out of the vehicle, you should require proper leash manners. You want to ensure your dog is exhibiting good self-control before being let free within a group of dogs.

To teach self-control while walking, use the "object of desire" exercise. In this case, the object of desire is the play area. Use a short leash and appropriate leash handling skills.[1] Keep your thumb tucked in your pocket or belt loop so you keep your arm at your side, and so you are not tempted to pull back on or correct the dog by "popping" the leash. Walk forward if the dog is not pulling on the leash. If he begins to pull, walk backwards until he is walking with you. At this point, you can move forward again until he pulls. During this exercise you are never stationary. The reward for the dog is getting to be closer to the object he desires (play area), while the consequence is having it taken away with distance. You can also use this exercise when the dog is approaching other dogs on leash or people. If you have to back up repeatedly, put the dog in a thirty second time-out back in the car, or at least out of sight of the play area. Once he is close to the gate, give him an audible "okay" and allow him to approach.

---

[1] Visit our YouTube channel to see this exercise

When at the gate require your dog to show self-control before giving permission to enter. This can be tricky because you don't want your dog meeting other dogs through the fence as this can cause barrier aggression. You may want to wait until the gate area is clear to begin the process and entering the "holding" area. If you are already in the "holding" area be sure to let your dog in as quickly as possible, preferably with the leash already off.

Make a point to interact with your dog during playtime. Anytime he comes by to check in with you praise him. Be sure to stick close by so you can let him know when he's exhibiting appropriate play behavior and so you can interrupt anything inappropriate. It is your responsibility to help him learn interaction skills.

Chapter 7
Working with Dogs With
Interaction Issues

Unfortunately, by the time a dog gets into his forever home, he may have missed ample opportunities to develop good social skills. He may suffer from leash reactivity, fear, phobias or aggression. Even if he's not an ideal candidate for play or interaction at this time, there are steps you can take to help him develop his skills and begin appropriately interacting with other dogs.

First, locate a positive trainer in your area who can walk with you through the process from beginning to end. In the meantime, begin working with your dog on the following:

Putting on a Muzzle

If your dog has any reactivity or aggression towards other dogs he must first become acclimated to a muzzle. There are two different types of muzzles. Mesh muzzles and basket muzzles (these remind people of Hannibal Lector's face contraption). I prefer basket muzzles, though many find it easier to give treats through a mesh muzzle. Regardless of which you choose, ensure it is fitted properly to prevent your dog from getting it off.

When the muzzle has been fitted properly, you begin associating good things with the muzzle so your dog is comfortable during training sessions. Ensure when the muzzle is in sight or on that your dog is constantly given treats. If you follow these steps your dog should be searching for the muzzle in order to earn yummy rewards. This must be done before working on any dog interaction related issues where aggression is involved.

1. Grab your muzzle and some of your dog's favorite treats. Boiled chicken works great for this. Present the muzzle to your dog and immediately give him a treat. Do this three times and then hide the muzzle behind your back. Ignore your dog while the muzzle is out of sight. Wait a few seconds and present the muzzle and treat again. Do this three more times and then hide the muzzle. Wait a little longer before repeating. Do this several times over the first day. You may also use other rewards such as tossing a ball when your dog sees the muzzle. Remember, when you are not working on this exercise to put the muzzle away.

2. The next day, repeat the above exercise three times or until your dog is completely relaxed when seeing the muzzle. Once he is, place the strap of the muzzle around your dog's neck and snap it while giving yummy rewards. Do not place the muzzle over your dog's snout at this time. Keep it on for 15-30 seconds, treating the entire time, and then remove it. Hide the muzzle behind your back and ignore your dog. If your dog becomes anxious at any time while wearing it, remove it immediately. Do short sessions,

several times on this day.

3. The next day, you will begin teaching your dog to place his snout into the muzzle. If using a basket muzzle, you may place treats inside the muzzle while cupping it into your hand so the treats don't fall out. Allow your dog to stick his nose in and retrieve the food. Before he is finished eating the treats remove the muzzle and hide behind your back. You will want to remove the muzzle from your dog before he moves himself away from it. If you are using a mesh muzzle, you may place a treat through one end using your fingers and require your dog to stick his snout in to retrieve it. Do not push the muzzle into your dog's face. Instead, allow him to approach it. Keep these sessions short but do them several times a day.

4. When your dog is comfortable with the above exercises, you will begin requiring your dog to keep his snout in the muzzle for longer amounts of time. Instead of the treats being inside the muzzle you will be feeding them through the front. You may want to use an easier treat source such as baby food or canned cheese for this exercise. Remember to remove the muzzle from your dog before he has a chance to move from it. When he seems comfortable with this, begin bringing the snaps of the muzzle together behind his head, without clicking or locking them into place. Pull them to the back of the head for 2-3 seconds while he is still eating the treat and give verbal praise. Drop the straps,

treat through the front of the muzzle and play with the straps again.

5. When your dog is comfortable with the step above you may begin clipping the straps behind his head. Keep them lose at this time. Continue rewarding him while the muzzle is clipped in place. You will want to remove it before your dog becomes too distracted by it. This may be no more than 10 seconds.

6. Lastly practice keeping the muzzle on for longer periods with more time in between rewards. You may feed your dog dinner, ask for particular behaviors or give treats while he is wearing it. You should begin increasing the time the muzzle is on your dog.

Additional Notes

- Never remove the muzzle if your dog is paying extra attention to it or attempting to get it off. Distract him and reward him while he is leaving it alone. Take it off only when he is not bothered by it. If he is bothered quickly, you may have moved too quickly through the steps.

- Put the muzzle on your dog at random times and not just when you need to work on dog interaction issue. This way, your dog will be less stressed and you can focus on rewarding appropriately.

- Allow your dog to control the speed at which you move through the above exercises. Forcing the muzzle on will create fear and a negative association.

Self-Control

Many dog interaction or aggression issues stem from a lack of self-control. When a dog feels overwhelmed, over-aroused or frightened, a lack of self-control will cause him to overreact instead of responding appropriately. You can work to improve your dog's self-control during his everyday routine.

To teach self-control, first identify what your dog views as rewards (e.g. going outside, coming inside, getting his leash on, going for a walk, getting dinner, etc.). In order for your dog to earn these rewards, he must display controlled excitement (four feet on the floor, with no excessive barking or "dancing"). Do not command your dog to act appropriately, but instead wait for him to display controlled excitement. When he does, give him permission to access his reward. This will take time as he learns what you expect from him. Remember to ignore him until he offers acceptable behavior.

Eye Contact

If you are unable to get your dog's attention it will difficult to improve your dog's behavior around other dogs. Begin in your home by using your dog's food as a reward. Sit down and say your dog's name. When he looks at you, give a verbal praise then a bite of food. Eventually, you can add a command such as "check in" or "look" with this exercise if you would like. Move around the house giving your dog the command and rewarding any eye contact. When he is proficient with this exercise at feeding time, begin practicing a random times throughout the day. Remember to give a yummy treat when he responds appropriately to his name or command. Slowly begin changing the location of this exercise and the predictability of rewards so you become like a "slot machine," only rewarding variably. This will keep him checking in. If he comes to you on his own throughout the day, be sure to give verbal praise and a sporadic treat.

Leash Manners

If your dog suffers from leash reactivity when around other dogs, he must first learn how to walk on a leash properly. There are several techniques for leash walking, but for this particular issue, I recommend changing direction when your dog pulls. This will help him learn to pay attention to you instead of the distraction. Be sure you have practiced building self-control with your dog prior to walks.

When walking your dog on a leash try to keep the leash loose. Do not use the leash to direct or correct your dog. Keep your leash hand next to your body, and put your thumb in a belt loop or pocket to prevent either. A waist leash can also assist with this.

Start practicing in your yard, and reward your dog anytime he stands nicely beside you. When he is relaxed, move a few steps in any direction and reward him for coming with you. Slowly integrate more steps in this process until you can walk your dog around your yard without him pulling.

For more tips on leash walking, you can purchase our book related to the subject on Amazon or our website.

Interruption Command

You must be able to stop your dog from continuing inappropriate behavior with just the sound of your voice, regardless if your dog is on or off leash. Refer back to the section in Chapter 2 regarding the split up technique. [2]

Begin this exercise in your home. If your dog ever spends time barking out a window, the front door or at your other dog or cat, he is giving you an opportunity to work on this exercise.

When your dog displays a behavior that needs to be interrupted, give him the command phrase ("that's enough") once, then use your body to "split-up" the action. You will face your dog, say nothing more, and move with him until he redirects and moves away. If you do this on a regular basis he will learn when he hears the command phrase he should move away or stop the behavior he is displaying.

---

[2] This exercise can also be seen on our YouTube channel.

Outside Help

It's not unusual for owners to need outside help with their dog's interaction issues. There are positive trainers and qualified daycares who can assist with your needs. Not all dog daycares are qualified, or interested, in helping your dog improve upon his social skills, so do some research to ensure he is in good hands. Not all daycares are equal so don't be afraid to be your dog's advocate.

Begin by finding a daycare that is clean and staffed properly, and also allows unscheduled tours and allows you to watch a playgroup (from a distance) before bringing your dog in for testing. The facility should have management that is capable of answering all your questions, without hesitation. For a guide, be sure to ask the following:

Chapter 8
Resources

This book is designed as a supplement to our seminar of the same name. You can locate this seminar online through our website or host a live one yourself. Dog Communication, which is covered in this book, is a separate seminar, and is a pre-requisite to the interaction seminar.

Website: www.dogspeak101.com

E-Training for Dogs: Bring Nikki's seminars, including "Understanding Dog Interaction" to your home! www.e-trainingfordogs.com

Facebook: Get the latest news from DogSpeak! www.facebook.com/DogSpeak101

YouTube: Check out exclusive training videos! www.youtube.com/DogSpeak102

Other guides and books are available at Amazon.com

Email: Info@dogspeak101.com

ABOUT THE AUTHOR

Nikki Ivey, Canine Behavioral Specialist, is the owner and founder of DogSpeak™. She has been working with dogs and their owners since 1996. She has spread her wealth of knowledge to not only the general public but to the professional pet world as well. She loves to educate individually and in groups, wanting all pet owners and professionals to have a better understanding of dogs and to have the healthiest possible relationship with them.

Nikki has spent many years learning to truly understand the nature of dogs and their motivations. By letting go of the "dominant pack theory" method, she is allowed to be more in tune with dogs, and more effective using her own method of training known as DogSpeak™. Nikki uses positive methods with negative punishment such as time-outs, stopping playtime and taking away attention. She doesn't use any form of physical correction such as correction collars, shock devices or fake bites. This allows dogs to show their true personality, builds their confidence and always leaves them happy. It also ensures that children aren't being taught to be negative or physical with their dogs when teaching.

Nikki believes in clearly communicating with dogs, setting their expectations and giving them a confident leader. She teaches foundation skills to dogs such as self-control and problem solving. Once a solid foundation is in place, you can begin to build the walls of real life manners that go beyond the traditional obedience training of sit, stay, down, come and heel. With real life manners your dog will know how to respond in situations without having to be commanded by you; however, when you do need to command your dog, they respond quickly and enthusiastically.

Nikki also owned and operated one of the first dog daycare in Middle Tennessee and has spent the last seven years helping others build their successful daycares, either from the ground up or as an additive to an existing business. She trains staff members on dog behavior and interaction at daycares, veterinary clinics and boarding facilities. Local rescue groups and shelters have also taken advantage of Nikki's classes to help their volunteers and foster parents understand the importance of dog communication and behavior to help place dogs into forever homes.

In 2001, Nikki founded Tennessee Emergency Rescue and Recovery Association (TERRA), which uses K9s to locate missing persons and deceased individuals in water or land. She's not only a handler of a Human Remains Detection dog but also teaches other handlers to work their dog in HRD.

In her spare time Nikki enjoys writing, and often incorporates her knowledge of search and rescue. Nikki's first novel, *Callout*, is available online at any large bookstore. Other training guides can be found through Amazon.

Made in the USA
Las Vegas, NV
30 November 2021

35658509R00039